Frederick O Layman

Views of prophecy concerning the Jews, the second advent and the millennium

Frederick O Layman

Views of prophecy concerning the Jews, the second advent and the millennium

ISBN/EAN: 9783337137618

Printed in Europe, USA, Canada, Australia, Japan

Cover: Foto ©Lupo / pixelio.de

More available books at **www.hansebooks.com**

VIEWS OF PROPHECY

CONCERNING

THE JEWS, THE SECOND ADVENT, AND THE MILLENNIUM.

BY A LAYMAN.

"King Agrippa, believest thou the Prophets?"

PHILADELPHIA:
SMITH, ENGLISH & CO.,
No. 23 NORTH SIXTH STREET.

NEW YORK: SHELDON & CO.—BOSTON: GOULD & LINCOLN.—
CINCINNATI: GEO. S. BLANCHARD & CO.

1866.

CONTENTS.

(iii)

PREFACE.

THIS little book contains the substance of a short course of lectures, delivered during the spring of the present year, to a limited audience, for whom exclusively they were prepared.

Some of the hearers, to whom the views were novel, expressed a wish to possess them in a permanent form for reference; and accordingly, at such leisure hours as I could command, this volume has been prepared for the press, including some points omitted in the delivery.

I am well aware that all it contains has been better said by others; but there appears to be yet room for a short elementary introduction to these momentous topics, and this has no higher pretensions.

My aim and desire are to induce the members of our churches, of every name, who have hitherto overlooked or neglected these subjects, to examine them heedfully and prayerfully for themselves. If true, they are certainly very important; and I hope to show that many of those who testify in their behalf are worthy, not only of a respectful, but of a reverential hearing.

To such of our clergy as violently oppose these ancient and venerable doctrines, I commend the words of the sage Gamaliel: "If this counsel or this work be of men, it will come to nought; but if it be of God, ye cannot overthrow it, lest haply ye be found to fight against God."

E. M.

September, 1865.

VIEWS OF PROPHECY.

CHAPTER I.

THE JEWS: THEIR PRESENT CONDITION, PAST HISTORY, AND FUTURE PROSPECTS.

THERE exists among us, and in all quarters of the world, a remarkable people, who without possessing a country, cling to their nationality; without the possibility of performing the most important rites of their religion, because these are forbidden except in a single place, which is not in their possession; they adhere pertinaciously to its mutilated forms. They have long controlled, in an important degree, the finances of nations which debarred them from the privileges of citizenship; and though mingling with us in social life, and in ordinary business transactions, they look with horror upon any marriage out of the pale of their own people. Their names continually remind us of the kings, heroes, poets, and prophets of the Old Testament; and their peculiar physiognomy

(7)

and strange customs plainly express, that although
with us, they are not of us.

We are so accustomed to look upon the Jews as
a weak and scattered people, that we forget their
great aggregate numbers, and also the influence
which they exert in consequence of their wide
dispersion. It is extremely difficult to obtain correct statistics in regard to them, and the estimates
of their aggregate numbers, made by different
writers, differ very widely. In a standard work,
"The Cyclopedia of Missions," by the Rev. Harvey
Newcomb, the whole number of Jews in the world
is estimated at 14,000,000, of whom, according to
the same authority, 5,000,000 are readily accessible
to missionary operations. These numbers can of
course be only approximate, but they are certainly
startling. Think of it. This scattered, despised
people, are probably equal in numbers to the whole
population of the United States in 1830; greater
than the entire population of Mexico and Central
America; greater than Spain; and nearly equal
to Belgium, Holland, Denmark, Sweden and Nor-
way combined. Nay, the Jews are probably more
numerous than they were when King David reigned
over them, in the height of his glory; for if we take
the number of fighting men counted by Joab at his
monarch's command (1 Chron. 21 : 5), 1,570,000,
and add one-fifth for the two tribes which were not
counted, and then suppose the non-combatants,
women, children and old men, to have been six

times as numerous as those able to bear arms, the total will be 13,188,000.

The influence which the Jews exert upon finances and trade — upon literature, science and the arts—would be an interesting theme, but not in accordance with my present object. I cannot refrain, however, quoting from an eloquent writer, in regard to Jewish influence upon the Christian world, the following passage:

"The European continental press is mainly in Jewish hands; every department of periodical literature swarms with Jewish laborers. The newspaper press is under their control, and the correspondence is mainly conducted by them. Taking a step higher, we find them again. We ask for knowledge of the mysteries of the starry heavens, and the children of Israel become our instructors. The Herschels and Aragos are the leaders of that lofty band of celestial travellers that journey among the stars. We cry for light upon the mysteries of revelation, and the children of Israel open the pearly gates of day, and light flows around us. Jahn, Hengstenberg, Tholuck, Krummacher, and a host of others, furnish us with biblical criticism, didactic theology, and general sacred literature. We ask for a key to unlock a dialect of Moses and the Prophets, and a Hebrew takes one from his drawer. Gesenius gives us our lexicon, and Nordheimer our grammar. We would have the dark chasm in early church history filled up, and a

bridge thrown across it, in order that we may pass
safely from inspired to uninspired history; the
children of Israel furnish the materials, and cover
the chasm.   Neander furnishes us with our incom-
parable Christian church history, and Da Costa
with a history of the Jews.   What need I add
more?   These facts show that the Hebrew intellect
is exerting a powerful influence upon the secular
and sacred literature of our age."

It is a melancholy truth, which we ought to
acknowledge with shame and confusion, that the
churches of America have come far short of their
duty in regard to Israel; and that, indeed, the
Jews are almost forgotten in our enterprises of
Christian benevolence.   It ought not to be so, for
our obligations to the ancient people of God are
incalculable.   Under Providence, we are indebted
to them for the only authentic history of God's
dealings with men, for the space of thirty-six centuries; comprising the most ancient literature in
existence, and the most sublime poetry the world
has ever produced.   Their watchful care and holy
reverence have preserved the Old Testament pure
and unmutilated, while so much of the literature
of Greece and Rome, comparatively modern nations, has perished forever.

Where is the literature of the great Empire of
Assyria, which once dominated the earth?   Layard
has groped among the ruins of Nineveh, and asto-
nished the world with the monstrous idols he has

discovered and dragged to light. He has copied the elaborate cuneiform inscriptions which cover the alabaster walls of the great palaces, so long buried beneath the earth, and thus preserved from decay; and he has distributed them among the learned men of Europe. All they have been able to read is worthless, and what they have hitherto been unable to read, may be more worthless still.

Of ancient Egypt numerous and magnificent monuments exist, attesting the vast wealth and power of a people who have passed away. Pyramids, the wonders of the world, built to eternize kings whose very names are in doubt; temples of a vastness that awes the beholder, covered with hieroglyphical writings, pictures and sculpture, which perplex philosophers, and which, when deciphered with infinite labor and skill, are found to be comparatively valueless, except as here and there they confirm the authenticity of the Hebrew record.

No trace now exists of these ancient and powerful nations, except their wonderful sculpture and architecture, the meagre historical records engraved on these remains, and statements concerning them in the Old Testament, which the Jews have preserved. The Jewish architecture has well nigh perished. Their glorious temple, the only place where they were permitted to offer the numerous sacrifices enjoined by their sacred law, was utterly destroyed by the Roman conquerors, eighteen cen-

turies ago. Its holy site is polluted by Mohammedan mosques, dedicated to the worship of a false
religion, and certain death awaits any Jew found
within their walls. But the Jewish people remain,
the best known, the most strongly defined race in
the world. They are scattered over the whole
earth, as their own inspired prophets of old pre-
dicted, and their present condition is a standing
miracle, a proof of the unfailing truth of God.

Shall it be always thus? Are the sins of the
parents to be visited on the children through all
generations? Is that sublime myth, "The Wandering Jew,"— who is said to have smitten the suffering Saviour, as he staggered under the weight
of the cross, on his painful journey from Pilate's
judgment-seat to Calvary, and who was condemned
for this horrible sin to walk the earth forever,
finding no rest for his weary body, and though
goaded continually by remorse, unable to repent,—
to be forever a type of the Jewish people?

Not so. The predictions of the Old Testament,
that the Jews as a nation are to be restored to
God's favor, to be reinstated in their own land,
and to be again God's chosen and beloved people,
are numerous, distinct and particular? I do not
hesitate to say, that if there is any fact clearly and
repeatedly recorded in prophecy, it is, that the
millennium for which we hope and pray, will not
come until the Jews as a nation, and in their own
land, are gathered into the fold of Christ. The

Apostle Paul affirms this restoration, and quotes
ancient prophecy to prove it (Romans, chap. 11).
The prediction to which he refers you will find in
Isaiah 59 : 20.   If you will read this with the context, to the end of the next chapter, which is a
part of the same prophecy, you will see that the
millennial glory is immediately to follow this restoration. This is only one out of a host of similar
predictions. In the Epistle referred to, the Apostle
tells the Gentile Romans, "blindness in part is
happened to Israel, until the fulness of the Gentiles be come in. And so all Israel shall be saved :
as it is written, there shall come out of Sion the
Deliverer, and shall turn away ungodliness from
Jacob : for this is my covenant with them, when I
shall take away their sins."

Although commentators have in so many cases
"spiritualized" the meaning of Israel, Jacob, and
Zion, insisting that these names, so full of meaning
to the Jews, only signify in prophecy the Christian
Church—I know of no one who has ventured to do
so in this instance ; for the contrast in the whole
passage, of which the above is a small part, between
the Gentiles, to whom the Apostle was writing, and
the Jews, of whom he wrote, utterly forbids such
interpretation.   Even Dr. Whitby, in regard to this
passage, speaking of the hope of the conversion
and restoration of the Jews, acknowledges : "It
hath been the constant doctrine of the Church of
Christ, owned by the Greek and Latin fathers, and

by all commentators I have met with on this place."

Dr. Burkitt says: "Hence it appears from the predictions of the prophets of God, that there shall be a general calling of the Jews to the faith of the Gospel, before the second coming of Christ."

Dr. Doddridge says: "As this Epistle was written long after the most remarkable conversion of the Jews by the first preaching of the Apostles, and, after St. Paul had been about thirty years engaged in his work, it appears that the prophecies relating to the calling of the Jews were not accomplished then, and consequently are not yet accomplished."

Dr. Scott says: "About the time of the last great harvest of the nations, the 'blindness' will be removed from Israel, and the nation saved from its rejected and dispersed state, and be brought in a body to embrace the Gospel; probably it will be restored to the Holy Land, and most of the Jews at least will become true believers."

Rev. Albert Barnes says: "In this manner, or when the great abundance of the Gentiles shall be converted, then all Israel shall be saved." "The time would come, when as a people they would be recovered, when the nation would be turned to God."

I close these citations with Dr. Hodge, of Princeton: "Israel here from the context must mean the

Jewish people, and 'all Israel' the whole nation, in opposition to the part spoken of above. Now, part of the Jewish people is rejected: then, the whole shall be gathered in. The nation as such shall acknowledge Jesus to be the Messiah, and be admitted into His Kingdom."

I once examined a learned and voluminous commentary on the Apocalypse, in which the author endeavored to prove that the millennium commenced a long time since, and is now in full career. Although this strange fancy has been held by various writers, ever since the days of Constantine, it can hardly be necessary to waste argument upon it in America. If the devil has been chained throughout the last four years, during the flagrant sins of the camp and the march, the bloody carnage of battles and sieges, the murderous massacres of the border guerillas, and the cruel tortures of Belle Isle and Andersonville, what can he do worse when "loosed for a season"?

There are but few professing Christians who do not expect and earnestly hope for a future millennium of some kind; and if it be true that the conversion and restoration of Israel must precede that event, we ought to be laboring faithfully to advance that conversion. Let the reports of our missionary boards, committees and societies, and the religious periodicals of all denominations testify, what slight efforts we are making for this object; and let every church member ask himself, how often he in his closet, or his pastor in the pulpit, earnestly prays for the salvation of God's ancient people? Our inexcusable apathy is one reason why we so rarely see or hear of a converted Jew; but there are other important reasons, which I will point out in another chapter.

CHAPTER II.

THE great stumbling-block in the way of the conversion of the Jews, in Romish countries, and in those which hold the Greek faith, is the idolatry of those called Christians. Scourged by their Divine Master for centuries, on account of their inveterate propensity to forget Him, and to worship idols of the heathen around and among them, the Jews now abhor the image and picture worship of nominal Christians, and their adoration of saints and angels and the Virgin. It is a sad fact, that 3,500,000 Jews who reside in those countries, look upon Christianity as synonymous with idolatry.

But there is also a stumbling-block in Protestant countries, and it behooves us seriously to consider it. The Jews look for the personal advent of the Messiah, to sit on the throne of his father David, to reign over Israel, and to be King of nations as he is King of saints. They point to a long list of unfulfilled prophecies of His glorious coming, and

2   2*   (17)

they find Protestant Christendom, to a great extent, busy in explaining away the meaning of these passages — interpreting Israel, Judah, Jacob, Ephraim, Jerusalem and Zion to mean merely the Christian Church, and the glorious promised kingdom of the Messiah to be nothing but the general spread of religion.

When our blessed Lord came in humiliation, to suffer and to die for sinful men, the Jews rejected him. Although the man of sorrows was so clearly and distinctly prophesied, with all the details of his sufferings and death, they could not recognize in him the triumphant Messiah, who was to come, glorious in apparel, travelling in the greatness of his strength, trampling the nations in his fury; the Redeemer who would build up Zion, and appear in his glory; who would assemble the outcasts of Israel, and gather the dispersed of Judah; who would break his enemies with a rod of iron, and dash them in pieces like a potter's vessel; who would reign in Zion and Jerusalem, and before his ancients gloriously. The veil was upon their hearts, and so they "spiritualized" or altogether neglected a large class of prophecies, which we know were not only substantially, but literally fulfilled. They could not understand, that the two sets of predictions which appeared irreconcilable and contradictory, related to two distinct advents. They could not perceive, that Christ must come in humiliation, and be offered up as a sacrifice, before he could come in glory, and receive the crown from His Father.

Are not we committing a similar error? What better right have we to explain away the predictions to which they cling, than they had to neglect or explain away those to which we point, as literal proofs of God's everlasting truth? Say not that such views are carnal. Do not we believe in the literal resurrection of the body? That Enoch walked with God, and was not, for God took him? That Elijah was taken up bodily by a whirlwind into heaven? Do we not boast of Immanuel, God with us, an incarnate Redeemer? Do we not believe that Christ was taken up bodily to heaven? And shall we not believe the words of the shining ones, who comforted his stricken disciples as they looked wistfully after their departed Master, with the words, "This same Jesus which is taken up from you into heaven, shall so come in like manner as ye have seen him go into heaven?" Is it more carnal to reign as a king, than to labor as a carpenter, or to be crucified as a malefactor?

With what assurance can we take up the Bible with an unconverted Jew, and say, "These prophecies must be interpreted literally, because we know that they have been literally fulfilled; but all the others relating to your nation must be interpreted 'spiritually,' or figuratively, because our best commentators do not believe they will ever be literally fulfilled?" May he not answer, as one

substantially did to an English clergyman, "You
only believe God's prophecies because you suppose
they have been fulfilled; we believe because *thus
saith the Lord!*"

That the early Christians, including the Apostles
and Evangelists, believed in the second personal
advent of the Messiah before the Millennium, seems
to me plain, both from the New Testament and
from church history. The coming of the Lord,
for which they were exhorted to watch, for which
they were to be always ready, for which they constantly prayed, was an actual personal coming,
which was to be sudden and unexpected: "Like
a thief in the night;" "like the lightning;" "in
an hour that ye think not." Trench well says in
his Commentary on the Epistles to the Seven
Churches: "Ever and ever in Scripture, not the
day of death, but the day of the Lord Jesus is put
as the term of all conflict." John has recorded an
unanswerable proof that the Apostles and their
associates had no idea that Christ's coming meant
death. When the Lord, after his own resurrection, foretold to Peter "by what death he should
glorify God," and Peter inquisitively asked, point-
ing to the beloved disciple John, "Lord, and what
shall this man do?" "Jesus saith unto him, If I
will that he tarry till I come, what is that to thee?
Follow thou me. Then went this saying abroad
among the brethren, that that disciple should not
die: yet Jesus said not unto him, he shall not die;

but, If I will that he tarry till I come, what is that to thee." So that instead of supposing that Christ's coming to a man meant death, the brethren supposed, and rightly, that if John should live until that coming, he would never die at all. Their mistake, which the Apostle corrects, was that they supposed the Lord had declared that John should tarry until his Master came back again to the earth.

The other common explanation, that the coming of Christ means the destruction of Jerusalem, is sufficiently refuted by the fact, that the Apocalyptic vision of John in the isle of Patmos, in which the Lord himself so plainly and solemnly encourages his faithful people, and warns the negligent and careless, by holding up this certain and inevitable coming before them, was witnessed and recorded more than a quarter of a century after Titus, with his Roman armies, had destroyed Jerusalem and carried the Jews into slavery.

Hear St. Paul's awful warning: "If any man love not the Lord Jesus Christ, let him be anathema maranatha." It is a pity our version does not translate these words. They mean "Let him be accursed, the Lord cometh."

The warning of St. Paul to the Thessalonians, that the day of Christ shall not come until after the Apostasy, and the revelation of the man of sin, who is to be consumed by the Lord with the spirit of his mouth, and destroyed with the brightness of his coming, shows conclusively, not only that the early Christians to whom he wrote, generally believed that the second advent was then instantly impending, but also that Paul himself believed and taught that it would certainly take place before the Millennium. If the man of sin be, as Protestant Christendom generally believes, some manifestation of the Papal power, that power is to exist until it shall be utterly destroyed by the *Epiphany of Christ's presence;* and certainly we cannot expect the Millennium until the mystery of iniquity is at an end.

I have touched lightly upon the belief of the early Christians, intending to return to it hereafter. It has drawn me from the consideration of the Children of Israel, to whom I return, by adopting the language of Dr. Horatius Bonar, of the Free Church of Scotland.

"The streams of the nations flow, tinged with drops from the cup of Israel: bright with her blessings, or discolored with her sorrows. All her invaders, from Shalmanezer to Titus, only dispersed her over the nations to exert a wider influence. The scattered dust of Samaria has sprinkled every nation of the East, and the exploded fragments of Jerusalem have found their way to every kingdom of the West. There are few nations or kingdoms that have not to some extent felt their silent passive influence. Like the Jesuits, though not with their accursed ends, they have influenced courts, and turned like a hidden rock, the currents of empires. Unnamed and unacknow-ledged, they have presided at royal councils. The financial prosperity of nations has taken its impulse from them, advancing or receding at their will. With the sinews of war in their hands, though with not even one soldier in the ranks, and with but little interest in the issue of the conflict, for whoever triumphed still they were oppressed, they waged war and made peace at pleasure. Theirs has been an influence everywhere felt, but nowhere acknowledged or honored; and in the midst of all this, suffering, torture, shame, and death have been the unvarying lot of the broken-hearted Jew. In what city have they not been dwellers, or sojourners at least, since first they ceased to have a city of their own? Whom have they not had for a sovereign since the day they cried, 'We will have no king but Cæsar?' They have seen no temple for many generations, since the hour when the Roman torch laid in ashes their beautiful house where their fathers praised; yet they hold fast their ancient worship, a spectacle of wondrous constancy, and blind fidelity stronger than death. No high priest has ministered at their altar since the time that Jerusalem was led captive; yet have they maintained their old tra-ditional religion, amid nations of infidels and idol-ators, in spite of everything that the torture or bribe could accomplish to make them renounce

their faith. What a monument! And who can
say how much the very sight of it has wrought in
the earth?

"Many a nation has been blest because they
favored Zion; but who has ever prospered that
injured her? He who has troubled her, has touched the apple of God's eye. Egypt was scourged
because she oppressed her. Edom was cursed and
plagued, because he remembered not the brotherly
covenant. Assyria was broken, because she overflowed Immanuel's land. Babylon was brought
low, because she held her in captivity. And soon
too shall mystic Babylon receive her awful recom-
pense for the blood and torture of the persecuted
race. It was an infidel king of the last century
that said, 'Meddle not with these Jews; no man
ever touched them and prospered.' Jerusalem has
truly been 'a cup of trembling to all people round
about, a burdensome stone for all people; and all
that burdened themselves with her have been cut
to pieces.'

"These are things which the Church of Christ
ought especially to remember, whether she considers the duty of favoring whom God favors, or
the blessing which he promises to those who seek
their peace, or the curses with which he has cursed
those who have trodden them down. Whether
then we call to mind the blessings which have
flowed from them to us, and see how their fall has
been our rising; or observe the manner in which

the prophets represent the future destiny of the
world as hanging upon the fortunes of Israel;
whether we remember their once high dignity, as
those to whom belonged the glory and the cove-
nants, the giving of the law and the promises, or
their long misery and degradation and dismember-
ment; whether we honor them as the kinsmen
of Christ, or pity them as the murderers of the
Lord of Glory; let us look upon Israel as God
looks upon her; let us understand the deep meaning of her history, and learn to sing her songs."

As Americans we have reason to be thankful,
that, many and grievous as the sins of our country
have been, for which we have of late years suffered
such sore chastisements, here at least the Jews
have never been persecuted. They have been
permitted to enjoy, not merely toleration, but the
full privileges of citizenship, and there are no
positions of honor or profit in our land to which a
son of Israel may not lawfully aspire. I shall
never forget a reply made by an intelligent Jewish
gentleman in my presence, twenty years ago, when
asked by a person abruptly, whether he believed
Messiah was yet to come? "No," replied he,
"America is our Messiah." Like very many of
his people here and in England, his religion was
only nominal, and the promised millennial blessings seemed to him sufficiently fulfilled in his com-
fortable American home. Sad as his infidelity
was, the reply contained an acknowledgement that

there is one deadly sin against God of which our nation is guiltless — the persecution of His ancient people.

In conclusion, if we are neglecting our duty in this regard, and thereby hindering the kingdom of Christ—if we have been ignoring the teachings of prophecy, and striving to do the Lord's work, not in accordance with His divine instructions and those of His inspired Prophets and Apostles, but of ingenious, though fallible, commentators—let us do so no longer.

May God give us all wisdom to understand the real meaning of His Holy Scriptures. May He teach us how to help His ancient people, and give us the heart to do so. May He take the veil away from their hearts, so that they may cheerfully abandon their self-righteousness and will-worship, and accept and rejoice in Jesus the true Messiah, who is at once the Lamb of God, who taketh away the sins of the world, and the Lion of the tribe of Judah; the Son of God, and the Son of Man; the suffering Saviour, and the conquering King; the root and the offspring of David; his Son and his Lord.

Blessed be His holy name for ever and ever. Amen.

CHAPTER III.

THERE is a method of interpreting Scripture which can make it mean whatever our fancies or our sentiments desire to find there. Origen, who flourished in the middle of the third century, is the great representative of this plan of interpretation, as well as the first prominent opponent of Millenarianism; which, as I hope to show hereafter, was the orthodox doctrine of the Apostolic church. Origen taught, that "the Scriptures were of little use, if we understand them as they were written;" that "words in many parts of the Bible convey no meaning at all;" that "the Scriptures are full of mysteries, and have a threefold sense, viz., a literal, a moral, and a mystical, and that the literal sense is worthless." He was claimed afterwards by the Arians, who denied the equality of Christ with the Father, as having taught their heresy; and he has also been claimed by the Universalists as belonging to them. They are welcome to him and his writings. It has been a great misfortune to the

(27)

church that he ever lived or wrote, notwithstanding his learning, his eloquence, and his martyrdom.

I hold that the Scripture is to be interpreted on the same principles as any other book written in a foreign language, in ancient times, viz.: by studying carefully what meaning the words would convey to those who received them. · And I accept as canons of interpretation the following: Luther says, "Let the Christian reader first seek to find out the literal meaning of the word of God; for this, and this alone, is the foundation of faith and of Christian theology." Hooker says, "I hold it for a most infallible rule in expositions of sacred scripture, that where a literal construction will stand, the farthest from the letter is commonly the worst."

Most writers, however, appear to think that the prophecies need not be interpreted literally, unless actual accomplishment compels it. In other cases there is a strong disposition to "spiritualize" the meaning, which often results in something entirely different from the plain text; and this, notwithstanding the acknowledged fact, that all the fulfilled predictions have been literally accomplished.

Theologians have adopted certain theories of their own, in regard to coming events, which they think are , more probable, more reasonable, and more spiritual than any other; and they have exhibited wonderful ingenuity, not in ascertaining what the book says, for that perhaps is plain enough, but in determining whether the words may not bear some other signification, more in accordance with their notions. This is a very dangerous mode of handling Scripture, for, having once accepted it, it is not easy to say "thus far thou shalt go and no farther." By a similar process the Unitarian begins by pronouncing the incarnation of Deity impossible, and vicarious atonement absurd; and his dreary task is to explain away the numerous passages in which these are affirmed, by assuming that the language is figurative; or, if this is impossible, he boldly pronounces them carnal, and rejects them as Jewish interpolations.

The Universalist cannot reconcile the mercy of God with the doctrine of everlasting punishment, and he disposes, in like manner, of the texts which interfere with his views.

Dr. Bush considers the resurrection of the body physically impossible, and removes troublesome passages which affirm it by a similar process.

The Quaker "spiritualizes" everything, rejecting the Lord's Supper, Baptism, Public Prayer, and what he calls a hireling ministry.

The Romanist teacher has a far more difficult task than any of these. His system is a wonderful and complex plan of man's device, overlaid upon God's work, and overshadowing it. He is compelled, therefore, to keep the Bible as far as possible a sealed book, and to let none of his people

3 *

read it without the notes and comments of the
Church, while he uses human traditions of apoc-
ryphal saints to reconcile the irreconcilable.

We have no difficulty in disposing of all these.
"To the Law and to the Testimony." We acknowledge no plenary inspiration, that is not contained
in God's word, and we accept that in its integrity.
God is truth. He is infinitely powerful, holy, wise,
just and good. There are many things which he
has revealed that we cannot fully understand, some
things which we cannot understand at all; but
everything which he has declared, we are bound to
believe implicitly. What is impossible with men
is possible with God. Our duty as Christians is
to endeavor humbly, earnestly, and prayerfully to
discover what "saith the Lord," and then to hold
fast to his words, remembering "that all Scripture
is given by inspiration of God, and is profitable for
doctrine, for reproof, for correction, for instruction
in righteousness; that the man of God may be perfect, thoroughly furnished unto all good works."
Especially in regard to prophecy, we should recol-
lect the emphatic words of the Apostle Peter:
"We have also a more sure word of prophecy,
whereunto ye do well that ye take heed as unto a
light that shineth in a dark place, until the day
dawn and the day star arise in your hearts: know-
ing this first, that no Scripture is of any private
interpretation, for the prophecy came not in old

time by the will of man; but holy men of God spake as they were moved by the Holy Ghost."

We should study the Scriptures, as far as possible, without any preconceived theories of what they ought to mean; and our great object should be to find out what they really do mean. When we find passages which apparently contradict each other, it may be necessary to search for a hidden meaning which does not appear on the surface; but in such cases, the general scope and teaching is to be assumed as the true one. We must not take isolated passages as proving facts or doctrines, which are elsewhere repeatedly denied, or clearly assumed to be false — as the Romanists find celibacy of their clergy in one text, purgatory in another, and the primacy of St. Peter in a third. The old dogma, that "where a text may be produced, there a doctrine may be founded," is a pernicious error, productive of evil and nothing but evil. Never was there a heresy yet, which could not quote Scripture in its defence, by this process of selecting particular passages and ignoring the general tenor and harmony of Scripture.

A portion of the prophetic books, and in an especial degree Daniel and the Apocalypse, contain symbolic representations of future events, which are apparently intended to be obscure and difficult of interpretation, until the time of their fulfilment. But this is not the case with regard to the whole of prophecy, nor even with regard to the principal part. Indeed, a very large portion requires to be examined, and its meaning determined, exactly as the narrative, didactic and historical portions of Scripture.

Let us take a few specimens to illustrate this, and they must be few comparatively, for the Bible is full of them, and our limits do not admit of an attempt to give the hundredth part of those that could be enumerated.

Ezekiel (26 : 3 to 5) prophesied concerning the great and wealthy maritime city of Tyre, as follows: "Thus saith the Lord God: behold I am against thee, O Tyrus, and will cause many nations to come up against thee, as the sea causeth his waves to come up. And they shall destroy the walls of Tyrus, and break down her towers: I will also scrape her dust from her, and make her like the top of a rock. It shall be a place for the spreading of nets in the midst of the sea; for I have spoken it, saith the Lord God; and it shall become a spoil to the nations."

Tyre was originally built on the sea-coast, and was afterwards extended to an island, a short distance from the mainland, which became the mart of the shipping. Nebuchadnezzar destroyed the old city on the mainland, with an army composed of many nations. Alexander the Great afterwards used the ruins to construct a causeway to the island, and scraped away the building materials, leaving the old city like a bare rock — fulfilling another prediction in the 12th verse of the same chapter: "They shall break down thy walls, and destroy thy pleasant houses; and they shall lay thy stones, and thy timber, and thy dust, in the midst of the water."

The capture of the insular city by Alexander was a blow from which Tyre never recovered. It often changed masters afterwards, was conquered and ruled successively by the Egyptian Ptolemies, by the Kings of Syria, by the Romans, by the Saracens, by the Christian crusaders, by the Egyptian Mamelukes, and last of all by the Turks — many nations thus literally making it a spoil, and aiding in the work of its destruction.

Of its condition, an intelligent traveller says: "On the north side it has an old Turkish ungarrisoned castle, besides which you will see nothing here but a mere Babel of broken walls, pillars and vaults, there being not so much as one entire house left. Its present inhabitants are only a few poor wretches, harboring themselves in the vaults, and subsisting chiefly on fishing, who seem to be preserved in this place, by Divine Providence, as a visible argument how God has fulfilled his word concerning Tyre, viz. that it should be as the top of a rock, a place for fishers to dry their nets on."

The Edomites were, as you all know, the descendants of Esau, the brother of Jacob. When the Israelites came up out of Egypt, the Edomites forgot the duties of kindred, and refused the wan-

derers, on their weary exodus, a passage by the
direct route through Idumea to the land of promise.
The permission was courteously asked, and a solemn pledge offered that no injury should be done
on the passage, but it was sternly refused. "And
Edom came out against him with much people, and
with a strong hand. Thus Edom refused to give
Israel passage through his border, wherefore Israel
turned away from him." For this and other sins,
God denounced against the Edomites the following
remarkable curse, by the mouth of his prophet
Isaiah, 34th chapter, 10th to 14th verse: "From
generation to generation it shall lie waste; none
shall pass through it forever and ever. But the
cormorant and the bittern shall possess it: the owl
also and the raven shall dwell in it; and he shall
stretch out upon it the line of confusion and the
stones of emptiness. They shall call the nobles
thereof to the kingdom, but none shall be there,
and all her princes shall be nothing. And thorns
shall come up in her palaces, nettles and brambles
in the fortresses thereof: and it shall be a habitation of dragons, and a court for owls. The wild
beasts of the desert shall also meet with the wild
beasts of the island, and the satyr shall cry to his
fellow: the screech owl also shall rest there, and
find for herself a place of rest."

As in the case of Tyre, the fulfilment of this
prediction must have appeared utterly impropable.
When these prophecies were uttered, Tyre and

Edom were at the height of their prosperity and power. And yet this denunciation also was literally fulfilled. For a great length of time Edom disappeared from among the nations, and was only known as a tradition or an historical remembrance. Numerous travellers endeavored to penetrate it without success, until 1818, when two Englishmen succeeded with great difficulty in reaching the chief city, Petra, where they found relics of the most extraordinary character of architecture, utterly desolate, frequented only by a few wandering Arabs, and inhabited by wild beasts and unclean birds and reptiles. So strange was the tale they told, that it seemed as if they had invented it to match the prophecy; and it was not until subsequent adventurers confirmed the truth of their story, that the London Quarterly Review ventured to use the following language:

"We have already said that we do not approve the zeal which endeavors by straining texts on one hand and facts on the other, to establish the literal accomplishment of what were probably meant as general denunciations; but it is remarkable that some of even the minutest circumstances of the Divine denunciations seem to be still in existence and operation. We do not doubt that the prophecy, being, as it unquestionably is, accomplished in all its parts, may be considered exhausted. The prophecy was pronounced against Edom, when it was a great and flourishing emporium, the heart and thoroughfare of all the traffic betwcen the Eastern and Western world: it was in that sense, and to that state of affairs, that the denunciation must have been pointed, and it was, when uttered, as significant in its local meaning, and as incredible as to its future accomplishment, as a similar interdict would now be against Cheapside, the Pont Neuf, or any other channel through which the great tide of human existence flows."

The prophecies concerning the children of Israel, are extremely numerous and in great detail. One element which they contain is very peculiar, and its fulfilment is patent to our eyes. They were to be terribly punished for their sins, but not destroyed. They were to be scattered among all nations, driven from their own land; but a remnant was to be preserved. You all know that this has been literally fulfilled. The preservation of a national character and national religion for eighteen centuries among a people without a country, dispersed over the whole earth, has well been called a standing miracle; and yet it was exactly what God said would happen.

But in immediate connection with these prophecies, and forming an integral part of them, are blessings of the most remarkable character, which are to follow their chastisements. I beg you to take your Bibles and read here before going farther, the following passages from eleven of the Old Testament prophets. They are so numerous that

the only difficulty is to make a selection, and I
have limited myself to only a single passage from
each, in order to show how they all concur in their
testimony:

Psalm 72, throughout; Isaiah 62, throughout;
Jeremiah 31 : 27 to 40; Ezekiel 37 : 15 to 28;
Hosea 3 : 4, 5; Joel 3 : 9 to 20; Amos 9 : 8 to 15;
Micah 3 : 8 to 4 : 7; Zephaniah 3 : 14 to 20; Hag-
gai 2 : 5 to 9; Zechariah 14, throughout. It
would be easy to multiply these quotations. Jeremiah and Ezekiel would furnish as many more;
and Isaiah alone, double the number I have enumerated; all bearing the same clear and distinct
testimony. The symbolical prophecies I have pur-
posely omitted, as you might have some doubts
about their meaning.

Study these writers for yourselves, and you will
find that the blessedness of Israel under Messiah's
reign, both temporal and spiritual, forms the burden of all their prophecies; and that although the
trumpet yields no uncertain sound, in regard to
the first coming of the Lord in humiliation, it rises
into strains of unparalleled sublimity, when it an-
nounces His second advent in glory.

I beg you also to notice, that these blessings are
promised to Israel and Judah, in exactly the same
manner as the curses are denounced against them,
and against Edom and Tyre. In some cases the
Gentiles generally, or specific nations, are mentioned in such connection as to shut up the pro-

4

mises to the Jews; and as these blessings are all
to follow the punishments which we know to be
now in progress and incomplete, and as we know
that hitherto the Jews have never enjoyed these
particular blessings, therefore they are yet unfulfilled.   But they will be accomplished.   What
God has promised will surely come to pass.   The
Lord my God shall come and all his saints with
him; His feet will again stand on the Mount of
Olives, and His ancient people will look upon
Him whom they pierced, and mourn and lament.
He will sit upon the throne of David and rule in
righteousness.   He shall set up an ensign for the
nations, and shall assemble the outcasts of Israel,
and gather together the dispersed of Judah from
the four corners of the earth.   Jerusalem shall be
a praise in the whole earth, for the mouth of the
Lord hath spoken it.

I will mention an instance of a strange perversion of an acknowledged figurative expression, in
order to draw your attention to the manner in
which we are in the habit of treating the prophetic
Scriptures.   How often in religious writings and
discourses the phrase, "treading the wine-press
alone," is applied to the Saviour's agony in the
garden and on the cross, when the light of His
Father's countenance was hidden from Him, and
He exclaimed in heart-piercing tones, "My God!
My God! Why hast thou forsaken me?"   The
passage is found in Isaiah, chap. 63, and means

exactly the opposite of the above sense. The
Messiah is described as triumphant, "glorious in
apparel, travelling in the greatness of His strength."
The prophet asks, "Wherefore art thou red in
thine apparel, and thy garments like him that
treadeth in the wine-fat?" And the response
comes, "I have trodden the wine-press alone, and
of the people there was none with me; for I will
tread them in mine anger, and trample them in
my fury; and their blood shall be sprinkled upon
my garments, and I will stain all my raiment.
For the day of vengeance is in my heart, and the
year of my redeemed is come. And I looked and
there was none to help: and I wondered that there
was none to uphold; therefore my own arm brought
salvation to me; and my fury it upheld me. And
I will tread down the people in mine anger, and
make them drunk in my fury, and I will bring
down their strength to the earth."

The apparent confusion of the present and future
tenses, arises from Isaiah seeing the future as if it
were present. This awful prediction exhibits the
triumphant Messiah singly, without assistance,
crushing the wicked nations, as the treader of the
grapes tramples them to pulp beneath his feet,
while their juice splashes over his garments.

The Apostle John, in the Apocalypse, describes
the same awful personage, and the same terrible
judgments in sublime language, and uses the same
expressive figure, wonderfully expressive in the

sense I have pointed out, but meaningless as usually
"accommodated."

"And he was clothed in a vesture dipped in
blood; and his name is called the Word of God.
And out of his mouth goeth a sharp sword, that
with it he should smite the nations: and he shall
rule with a rod of iron. and he treadeth the wine-
press of the fierceness and wrath of Almighty
God." The vesture dipped in blood here, does not
refer, as sometimes explained, to his own sacrifice,
but like the stained garments in Isaiah, to the
blood of his obdurate foes. The two prophecies
are identical, and an examination of the context
of each shows that they form a part of the terrible
scenes by which the millennium is to be ushered
in, and to which, in these last days, we are rapidly
drifting.

"Yet, once again thy sign shall be upon the heavens dis-
      played,
And Earth and its inhabitants be terribly afraid;
For not in weakness clad thou com'st, our woes, our sins to
      bear;
But girt in all thy Father's might, his vengeance to declare.

"The terrors of that awful day, oh! who can understand?
Or who abide when Thou in wrath shall lift Thy Holy Hand?
The Earth shall quake, the sea shall roar, the sun in heaven
      grow pale,
But Thou hast sworn and wilt not change, thy faithful shall
      not fail."

The eloquent and evangelical Doctor Horatius

Bonar has well said: "In so far as prophecy has
been already fulfilled, that fulfilment has been a
literal one. Take the predictions regarding the
Messiah. His being born of the house of David
of a virgin, at Bethlehem; being carried down to
and brought up out of Egypt; his healing diseases; his entering into Jerusalem on an ass; his
being betrayed by one of his disciples; his being
left by all his familiar friends; his being smitten,
buffeted, spit upon; his side being pierced; his
bones unbroken; his raiment divided by lot; his
receiving vinegar; his being crucified between two
thieves; his being buried by a rich man; his lying
three days in the tomb; his rising on the third
day; his ascending up on high, and sitting at the
right hand of God; these, and many others, have
all been fulfilled to the very letter — far more
literally than we could ever have conceived. And
are not these fulfilments strong arguments in favor
of the literality of all that yet remain behind?
Nay, do they not furnish us with a distinct, unam-
biguous, and inspired canon of interpretation?
Take, again, the prophecies which concern the
heathen nations — Babylon, Nineveh, Tyre, Moab,
Ammon, Edom, Egypt. Have not all these been
literally fulfilled? Or lastly, take the predictions
regarding Israel. Have not all been literally veri-
fied? Captivity, dispersion, exile, misery, contempt
and oppression, have been their history to this very
hour. And was there one particular of all their

wondrous history which prophecy did not foretell?
Up to this hour all has been literal fulfilment in
their case. And shall the curse pronounced on
them be fulfilled to the very letter, but not the
blessing?"

Let me quote another able writer, the Rev. J. C.
Ryle, of Christ's church, Oxford:

"It is high time for Christians to interpret
unfulfilled prophecy by the light of prophecies
already fulfilled. The curses on the Jews were
brought to pass literally; so also will be the
blessings. The scattering was literal; so also will
be the gathering. The pulling down of Zion was
literal; so also will be the building up. The
rejection of Israel was literal; so also will be the
restoration.

"It is high time to interpret the events that shall
accompany Christ's second advent by the light of
those accompanying his first advent. The first
advent was literal, visible, personal; so also will
be the second. His first advent was with a literal
body; so also will be his second. At his first
advent the least predictions were fulfilled to the
very letter; so also will they be at his second.
The shame was literal and visible; so also will be
the glory."

Amen! Even so, come, Lord Jesus.

CHAPTER IV.

PROPHECIES OF CHRIST'S COMING, FROM THE NEW TESTAMENT —
SIGNS OF THE TIMES IN REGARD TO A SPIRITUAL MILLENNIUM.

IT is not necessary to prove that the Jews, at the time of Christ's first advent, were expecting the coming of Messiah — not as he did come, in humiliation — but in great power and glory, to crush their enemies, and to restore the kingdom of Israel. They still wait and expect that glorious coming. The disciples of our Lord were Jews, and shared in the hopes and expectations of their people. Seeing his miracles, hearing from his lips such words as man never spake, they followed, loved, confessed him; but never ceased, until his death, to expect that he would in due time assume the throne of David his father. They could not, or would not understand, his distinct, repeated declarations, that "the Son of Man must suffer many things, and be rejected of the elders, and of the chief priests and scribes, and be killed, and after three days rise again."

At his crucifixion their hopes were dashed to the ground, and in despair they forsook him and

(43)

fled. But after his resurrection, the same idea per-
vaded their minds; and until he left them again
and ascended to heaven, they still expected. his.
assumption of the throne, and the re-establishment
of the kingdom.   Let us consult the word of God,
to see the Saviour's mode of correcting their errors
on this point.

When Peter, speaking for all the twelve, asked
the Lord what their reward should be for having
left all and followed him, Jesus answered: " When
the Son of Man shall sit on the throne of his glory,
ye also shall sit upon twelve thrones, judging the
twelve tribes of Israel."   Now, it is very easy to
understand how the Apostles shall, in the personal
millennial reign of Christ on the earth, hold literally and specifically the position of Judges or
Rulers over the. twelve tribes of Israel.   But I
must confess my own utter inability to conceive
of any other sense in which this can be said at all.
Very soon after, and evidently in reference to this
positive promise, James and John endeavored to
get from him a pledge, that they should have the
posts of chief honor among the Apostles, the seats
at his right and left hand in his glory.   Jesus did
not tell them they were in error, in regard to the
reality of the kingdom they were expecting, but
simply, " to sit on my right hand and on my left
is not mine to give, but it shall be given to them
for whom it is prepared of my Father."

Again, on the day of his resurrection, when the

two disciples, not recognizing their Master, sadly
told him of his own sufferings and death, which
they supposed to be the end of their cherished
hopes, adding, "But we trusted that it had been
He which should have redeemed Israel." Did he
tell them that Israel was not to be redeemed? No.
"He said unto them, O fools and slow of heart to
believe *all* that the Prophets have spoken!" They
did as we have been doing, believed a part and
overlooked or explained away the rest. "Then
beginning at Moses and all the Prophets, he expounded to them *in all the Scriptures*, the things
concerning himself." O that we had a record of
that Divine and infallible exposition! As we have
it not, we can only judge what it was by its effects.
They "returned to Jerusalem and found the eleven
gathered together, and them that were with them,"
and "they told what things were done in the way,
and how he was known of them in breaking of
bread." Having thus made their full report, they
appear, from Luke's narrative, to have remained
with the Apostles until their Lord's ascension.
And yet, after our Lord had remained forty days
on earth "*speaking of the things pertaining to the
kingdom of God,*" the very last question which his
assembled disciples asked him was, "Lord, wilt Thou
at this time restore again the kingdom of Israel?"
Now, I beg you especially to note, that this question was asked after Luke tells us expressly "then
opened he their understanding, that they might

understand the Scriptures." And his reply just
before his ascension to heaven in their presence
was, " It is not for you to know the times and the
seasons, which the Father hath put in his own
power." He does not say, " Your views are carnal,
there is to be no such restoration of Israel as you
anticipate; the prophecies you rest upon, only
mean that Christianity is to be greatly or universally extended." On the contrary, he assumes
their views to be substantially correct, but tells
them that it was not proper that they should know
the times and seasons when the restoration should
take place.

The parable of "the pounds" was uttered "because he was nigh unto Jerusalem, and because
they thought that *the Kingdom of God should immediately appear.*" In this parable, a nobleman going
into a far country to receive for himself a kingdom, places a sum of money in the hands of each
of his ten servants, to be used for his benefit
during his absence, with the command, "Occupy
till I come." Part of the citizens hating him,
announce their determination not to submit to his
authority. Upon his return, after having received
the regal dignity, he examines the accounts of his
servants, rewards the diligent according to the
measure of their faithfulness; punishes the slothful servant, who had not improved the opportunity
of serving his master, and then destroys his

enemies who had refused in advance to acknowledge his sway.

When we take into consideration the reason
assigned for the utterance of this parable, its meaning is obvious. The disciples supposed he was
going then to Jerusalem to assume kingly power,
to establish Messiah's kingdom, to ascend the
throne of David. To correct their erroneous im-
pressions, he does not tell them there is to be no
such kingdom; but that it is to be postponed, that
he must depart and be absent for a time to receive
the investiture of royalty, and that his servants
must labor diligently in his cause during his
absence. But that he would return with the glory
and power they expected in due time, reward the
faithful, rebuke the slothful, and destroy his
enemies.

It is repeatedly declared in the Bible, that Messiah is to sit upon the throne of David. He certainly did not do so when upon earth, and surely
the throne upon which he now sits at the right
hand of the Father, is not in any sense the throne
of David. David's throne is figurative, of course,
for David's kingdom; but that was a literal kingdom over the Jewish people, not a throne in
heaven. And with what propriety can we "spiritualize" this oft-repeated expression, which had so
plain a meaning for the Jews, to whom it was
spoken, and say David's throne, when applied to
the Messiah, only means that he will rule in the

hearts of Christian people, which never was David's prerogative. We might as well express the universal respect felt for Washington throughout the civilized world, by saying, that he sits on the throne of the Cæsars.

Christ's people are repeatedly commanded to wait and watch for the coming of the Lord. If there is to be a Millennium of blessedness before his coming, they may wait and watch for that; and O, how difficult it is, in these sad times of violence and infidelity, for faith to grasp and hold fast to the hope of the world's regeneration, without Messiah's presence! But how can they watch for a coming which is more than a thousand years off, and cannot come in their brief lives?

And where do we find the signs of that spiritual Millennium, which we have been fondly expecting would gradually extend until it covers the whole earth, as the waters cover the sea. Surely not in our own land, polluted with the crimes and cruelties of four sad years of war, during which the ground has trembled under the tramp of armed millions doing the work of death, and man's ingenuity has been exercised in devising new weapons and engines of destruction, more terrible than the world ever saw before. We have struck the shackles from the slave, but not for Christ's sake. We have crushed a wicked and causeless rebellion, but we had to wade through a sea of blood to victory. Does this look like turning the sword to the ploughshare, and the spear to the pruning hook, and men learning war no more?

Do you know the rate at which Romanism is growing in this country? An article written by M. Rameur, from materials obtained while travelling in America, originally published in France, but translated and republished here in the "Catholic World," contains the following statistics:

The ratio of Roman Catholics to the whole population, was, in 1784, 1 to 100; in 1808, 1 to 65; in 1830, 1 to 29; in 1840, 1 to 18; in 1850, 1 to 11; in 1860, 1 to 7. In 1784, there were from 30 to 40 priests; in 1808, 68 priests and 4 bishops; in 1830, 232 priests and 12 bishops; in 1840, 482 priests and 15 bishops; in 1850, 1800 priests and 31 bishops; in 1860, 2235 priests and 43 bishops.

M. Rameur gives the whole number of Romanists in 1860, as 4,400,000. By the census, the entire population of the United States, including negroes and Indians, was 31,443,332. In the Southern States they form only a tenth of the population, the negroes being generally Protestant; but in the Northern States they are one-sixth. While the Romanists increased in each decade 80, 125, and 109 per cent., other denominations increased only $20\frac{1}{4}$ per cent. The author says the conversion of Protestants is very considerable, the Episcopalians and Unitarians providing the largest number, and the Baptists and Methodists the least. He alludes to mixed marriages, and educational establishments

4   5

under church control, as aiding the church; and
expresses the opinion, that the ratio of growth
would be doubled if a sufficient number of ecclesi-
astics and missionaries were provided. Does this
look like a gradual progress to the Millennium?

If we turn our eyes to Protestant England, and
listen to the voices of her faithful sons, what do
they tell us? In London, the great heart of the
country, where more than two millions of people
are gathered together, in all the places of public
worship, Romanist and Protestant, including the
Established Church and Dissenters of every name,
there are not church sittings for one-fourth of the
population; not more than one-tenth frequent any
church at all, and the whole number of Protestant communicants does not exceed three per cent.
The statistics of London show, 3000 receivers of
stolen goods; 4000 are annually committed for
crimes, there are 10,000 gamblers, 20,000 habitual
beggars; 30,000 thieves, 150,000 habitual gin
drinkers, and 150,000 of both sexes who lead a
life of debauchery and licentiousness. Romanism
has increased in England since 1835 in a most
alarming degree, and the late Cardinal Wiseman
had reason to boast of his success, when he pointed
to the Papal churches, nunneries, monasteries, and
chapels built under his management, and to the
great increase of priests and perverts, as proof that
England was returning to the bosom of the Romish
Church.

Need I say anything of the manner in which the Puritans of New England and Old England have lapsed into Unitarianism? Of Newman, with the Tractarian party; and Colenso, with his followers, in the English establishment? Of the present phase of infidelity in England and America—that of science, falsely so called, more dangerous, in my judgement, than any former device of . Satan? Of Mormonism, Socialism, and Spiritualism, with their kindred abominations?

Shall we look at Continental Europe? Alas! "The Scribes and Pharisees sit in Moses' seat." Renan and Strauss are more quoted among nominal Protestants than Calvin or Luther; infidelity is rife even in the birth-place of the Reformation; a very large part of the continent is as truly missionary ground as Africa or Asia; and a multitude of those who believe not in the Pope believe in nothing.

The heart sickens when we think of the hundreds of millions, in heathen and Mohammedan countries, who have never heard of the Gospel of Christ; in whose borders the self-denying missionaries, laboring in season and out of season, can only here and there kindle a spark of celestial light on the surface of an ocean of darkness.

I know that the Pope trembles on his throne; and holds the feeble tenure of his power at the will of the inscrutable ruler of the Tuilleries. But what if that man of dark and mysterious purposes, when the frail old man who wears the triple crown shall pass away, should invest some puppet of his own with the tiara, and through him wield the Papal power throughout the world? Would not Romanism be like the man from whom one demon had been exorcised, only to readmit him with seven other demons more wicked than himself? *May not this indeed be the very Antichrist?*

Alas for Christendom! if we should be left to our own devices. We are crying Peace! Peace! when there is no peace. But, blessed be God, we shall not be left to ourselves. "When the enemy shall come in like a flood, the spirit of the Lord shall lift up a standard against him, and the Redeemer shall come to Zion, and unto them that turn from transgression in Jacob, saith the Lord." "And then shall that wicked be revealed, whom the Lord shall consume with the spirit of his mouth, and destroy with the brightness of his coming." "The day cometh that shall burn as an oven; and all the proud, yea, and all that do wickedly, shall be stubble; and the day that cometh shall burn them up, saith the Lord of hosts, that it shall leave them neither root nor branch. But unto you that fear my name, shall the Sun of Righteousness arise with healing in his wings; and ye shall go forth and grow up like calves of the stall. And ye shall tread down the wicked, for they shall be ashes under the soles of your feet, in the day that I do this, saith the Lord of hosts."

CHAPTER V.

IN an excellent book, entitled "Synonyms of the New Testament," written by the learned Dr. Trench, now Archbishop of Dublin, he points out a confusion of meaning which has arisen in consequence of our translators having unfortunately used a single English word, "world," to signify the meaning of two Greek words, *aion* and *kosmos*; the first of which has reference to time or duration, and the latter to material space. Trench regrets that they have not been distinguished by the words age and world; and says, "In all those passages which speak of the end of the aion (or age), *there are none that speak of the end of the kosmos* (or world); as in others which speak of the wisdom of the world, the God of this world, the children of this world, it must be admitted that we are losers by the course we have adopted." This is most true. If our translation read, as it should read, "The field is the *world*, the enemy that sowed them (the tares) is the devil; the harvest is the end of the *age*, and the reapers are the angels;" and if a like construction

5 *　　　　　　　　　　　　(53)

had been put on similar texts, readers unacquainted with Greek would not have concluded that the coming of Christ in the clouds of heaven, with His saints and angels, is to be accompanied or followed by the destruction of the material universe.

There is no good reason to believe from Scripture, that this earth will ever be destroyed; but many, very many positive texts which teach us that it will endure forever as the abode of the saints. Take these for example, you may find plenty more by searching for them: "The world also is established that *it cannot be moved.*" "Who laid the foundations of the earth, that it should *not be removed forever.*" "The earth which He has *established forever.*" "One generation passeth away and another generation cometh, but *the earth abideth forever.*" "Thy people shall be all righteous; they shall *inherit the land forever.*" "Look upon Zion the city of our solemnities: thine eyes shall see Jerusalem a quiet habitation, a tabernacle that shall not be taken down; not one of the stakes thereof *shall ever be removed,* neither shall any of the cords thereof be broken." "They that trust in the Lord shall be as Mount Zion, which cannot be removed, but *abideth forever.*" "And they shall dwell in the land that I have given unto Jacob my servant, wherein your fathers have dwelt: and they shall dwell therein, even they, and their children, and their children's children *forever:* and my servant David shall be their prince *forever.* More-

over, I will make a covenant of peace with them;
it shall be an everlasting covenant with them; and
I will place them, and multiply them, and will set
my sanctuary in the midst of them *forever more.*"
"Those that wait upon the Lord, they shall *inherit
the earth.*" "But the meek *shall inherit the earth,* and
shall delight themselves in the abundance of peace."
"For such as be blessed of him, *shall inherit the earth.*"
"The righteous *shall inherit the earth, and dwell therein forever.*" "Blessed are the meek for *they shall inherit the earth.*" "Thou hast made us unto our God
Kings and Priests, and *we shall reign in the earth.*"

Will any one pretend that these prophecies have
been fulfilled? that the righteous; those that wait
upon the Lord; they that trust in the Lord; the
meek; such as are blessed of the Lord; and above
all, those whom John saw in Apocalyptic vision
falling down before the Lamb with harps and
golden vials full of odors, which are the prayers of
the saints, and who sang the new song, have yet
inherited or reigned in the earth?   But we are
assured that they shall not only do so, but shall
dwell therein forever.

Although Peter says, "Seeing then that all
things shall be dissolved, what manner of persons
ought ye to be, in all holy conversation and godli-
ness, looking for and hasting unto the coming of
the day of God, wherein the heavens being on fire
shall be dissolved, and the elements shall melt
with fervent heat;" he adds immediately, "Never-

theless we according to His promise look for new
heavens and a *new earth*, wherein dwelleth righteousness." The best explanation of the apostle's
meaning is given by himself in a previous portion
of the same chapter, where, speaking of Noah's
flood, he says, "The world that then was, being
overflowed with water *perished.*" As the old world
defiled with sin perished by water, destroying the
obdurate sinners who then rejected the Lord, *so,
and not otherwise,* the present world will, when
Christ shall come in judgment, perish by fire, destroying the obdurate sinners who shall then reject the Lord. But as the old world emerged from
the water, so shall the present world emerge from
its fiery baptism — redeemed, regenerated, holy,
pure, and beautiful as it came from the hand of its
Maker before sin defiled it. Let those of my
readers who think this strange doctrine, read what
the eminent Dr. Chalmers says on the subject.
"The common imagination that we have of Paradise, on the other side of death, is that of a lofty
ærial region, where the inmates float in ether, or
are mysteriously suspended upon nothing; where
all the warm and sensible accompaniments, which
give such an expression of strength and life and
coloring to our present habitation, are attenuated
into a sort of spiritual element, that is meagre, and
imperceptible, and utterly uninviting to the eye
of mortals here below; where every vestige of materialism is done away, and nothing left but un-

earthly ecstacies, with which it is found impossible to sympathize." " We hail the information of our text, that after the dissolution of the present frame-work, it will again be varied and decked out anew in all the graces of its unfading verdure, and of its unbounded variety; that in addition to our direct and personal view of the Deity when he comes down to tabernacle with men, we shall also have the reflection of him in a lovely mirror of His own workmanship; and that instead of being transported to some abode of dimness and mystery so remote from human experience as to be beyond all comprehension, we shall walk forever in a land replenished with those sensible delights, and those sensible glories, which, we doubt not, will lie most profusely scattered over 'the new heavens and the new earth wherein dwelleth righteousness.'

" There will be a firm earth as we have at pre-sent, and a heaven stretched over it as at present; and it is not by the absence of these, but the ab-sence of sin that the abodes of immortality will be characterized. There will be both heavens and earth in the next grand administration, with only this speciality to mark it from the present one, that it will be a heaven and earth wherein dwelleth righteousness."

I have quoted Dr. Chalmers on this point at some length, because I presume his orthodoxy will not be questioned. How differently his language sounds from the fashionable teaching of the present day, which assigns such immediate, perfect, ineffable spiritual blessedness to the disembodied souls of those who have died in Christ, that it is difficult to look upon a future reunion with our bodies, in any other light than as a calamity. His faith was that of the saints and martyrs of the early church, who have left their testimony in the Roman catacombs. Among the almost countless inscriptions on their tombs, we are told that the word *death* never appears. All of them "sleep in Jesus." The hope which sustained them in persecution, was the resurrection of their bodies at Christ's coming. They knew that the seer of Patmos "heard a voice from heaven, saying, Write blessed are the dead which die in the Lord; yea, saith the Spirit, that *they may rest from their labours*." They confidently expected this blessed rest, but they knew also, that the same prophet in Apocalyptic vision "saw under the altar, the souls of them that were slain for the word of God, and for the testimony which they held; and they cried in a loud voice, saying, How long, O Lord, holy and true! dost thou not judge and avenge our blood on them that dwell on the earth? And white robes were given unto every one of them; and it was said unto them *that they should rest yet for a little season*, until their fellow servants also, and their brethren, that should be killed as they were, should be fulfilled." And they also knew, that when John saw "the Lion of the tribe of Judah, the Root of David," take the sealed book from the hand of His Father, "they sang a new song, saying, Thou art worthy to take the book and to open the seals thereof, for thou wast slain, and hast redeemed us to God by Thy blood out of every kindred, and tongue, and people, and nation: and hast made us unto our God kings and priests, *and we shall reign on the earth.*" The early church did not expect perfect bliss, until their bodies should arise from their sleep in the dust. Such was the teaching they received from the Apostles, and accordingly they embodied in the earliest Christian creeds the doctrine of the resurrection from the dead, as an essential article of faith. In attempting to be wise beyond what is written, we have devised an ideal future state, which has no scriptural warrant.

The editor of a prominent Episcopal journal in the United States, uses the following language:

"The Congregational paper of Illinois has been writing systematically against the resurrection and the general judgment for months past, and we have heard no word of warning or protest. It has declared that there is no resurrection of the flesh, in so many words; that the soul's going to heaven immediately after death, is all there is. The body is not needed at all." "The common teaching about the state after death, that the good go at once to heaven and the bad at once to hell, has made the resurrection superfluous, and led to the denial of its existence. Why bring a saint of five

thousand years' standing out of heaven, or a sinner
of as many out of hell, to go through the farce of
a judgment, or to receive the useless clog of a
body? In truth, we question seriously whether
the mass of the members of the so-called 'Evangelical Churches,' are not utter unbelievers in that
article of the creed, 'I believe in the resurrection
of the body.'"

I was not before aware that any organ of the
"so-called Evangelical Churches" thus formally
denied one of the great cardinal doctrines of Christianity, but it is by no means surprising. The
Episcopal editor could easily satisfy himself, that
great numbers of his own denomination, although
declaring verbally every Lord's day their belief in
the "resurrection of the body," really look upon it
as a mystical matter, by no means essential to
their future happiness; and this is a legitimate
result of the "spiritualizing" method of interpretation.

The parable of the rich man and Lazarus, does
not contradict our ancient and venerable doctrine,
as some suppose. Lazarus reposing in Abraham's
bosom, is typical of that blessed rest in which the
souls of believers wait for the resurrection; the
paradise of the repentant thief on the cross; as
Archbishop Trench expresses it, "the state of pain-
less expectation, of blissful repose, which should
intervene between the death of the faithful in
Christ Jesus, and their perfect consummation and

bliss at His coming in His glorious kingdom." And the rich man, by an unfortunate confusion of two distinct words, said to be in hell, is in hades, "the place of painful restraint, where the souls of the wicked are reserved to the judgment of the great day; it is the deep, whither the devils prayed that they might not be sent to be tormented before their time." The real Hell is the Lake of Fire, into which Death and Hades are to be cast at the great day of Final Judgment, after the resurrection of the wicked dead.

I suppose many Christians have been perplexed about the raising of the other Lazarus from the dead. We have every reason to believe that the brother of Martha and Mary was a true believer, for "Jesus loved Martha and her sister and Lazarus;" and when he wept at his tomb, "then said the Jews, behold how he loved him." Is it conceivable that the omniscient, benevolent Saviour would have recalled his beloved friend from the glory and perfect bliss of heaven, and compelled him to take up again his earthly burden, his body subject to sickness, and pain, and sorrow, even for the purpose of comforting the sisters, or of exhibiting His own power over death? I can hardly suppose this to be true, unless God said it, for it would *appear* to be cruelty not mercy; and I rejoice that it is not taught in the Bible.

CHAPTER VI.

THOSE who oppose the doctrine of Christ's personal reign on earth during the Millennium, rely greatly upon two texts: "My kingdom is not of this world," and "the kingdom of God cometh not with observation; neither shall they say, Lo here! or Lo there! for behold the kingdom of God is within you."

When Christ uttered these words to Pilate and to the Pharisees, although truly a King, he was a king in disguise. He has not yet ascended the throne of David and restored the kingdom of Israel. We still pray as he taught us, "Thy kingdom come;" that he will hasten his coming and kingdom; that he will reign King of nations; but he was then, is now, and ever shall be King of saints. He reigns now in the hearts of his people, but hereafter "*the kingdoms of this world* will become the kingdom of our Lord Christ." His present kingdom in Christian hearts "cometh not with

(62)

observation," but hereafter "as the lightning that lighteneth out of the one part under heaven shineth unto the other part under heaven; so shall also the Son of man be in his day." "Then shall they see the Son of man coming in a cloud with great power and glory." "The Lord himself shall descend from heaven with a shout, with the voice of the Archangel and the trump of God." "The Lord Jesus shall be revealed from heaven with his mighty angels." There is no contradiction between these texts and those before mentioned when properly considered and compared; and we should be careful not to quote the first in opposition to what the Spirit has elsewhere plainly spoken.

Among the many objections made to the literal interpretation of the Scriptures, none is more frequently insisted upon than its tendency to paralyze missionary operations. Our doctrines have no such tendency. Our blessed Lord's last command was, "Go! preach the gospel to all nations;" and on a former occasion he had declared, "This gospel of the kingdom shall be preached in all the world for a witness unto all nations; *and then shall the end come.*" Wo to us if we do not cause this gospel to be preached! We must see to it that the glad tidings of salvation are offered to every nation, and kingdom, and people under heaven, and the sooner we do this the sooner Christ will come; but *"when the Lord cometh shall he find faith on the earth?"* We have no promise that the world is to be converted by or through our efforts; nor is there any more reason from the Word of God to believe this, than that in any particular congregation in this city every individual who listens to the faithful preaching of his pastor will be truly converted. Would this excuse that pastor from laboring, striving, and praying for their salvation? If he does not, their blood will be upon his skirts. Not long since an eminent theological professor urged this objection to pre-millenarianism in an argument to his class, and few of them could resist a smile. They knew that only four of their number had devoted themselves to the cause of foreign missions, and of these three were pre-millenarians.

Oh no! bring not this charge against us. If all Christendom at this time earnestly believed that the Lord Jesus will soon come to judgment, *and that he may come to-morrow;* instead of our virtually saying, "Where is the promise of his coming?" or, "My Lord delayeth his coming;" think you we should not be fully awake and thoroughly in earnest to do his work? I tell you, the accumulated wealth of the whole church would be poured forth like water, in order to carry the gospel of the kingdom to the dark corners of the earth; missionaries would rush forward in crowds to gather in the harvest of the nations; to hasten the fulness of the Gentiles; to make ready a people prepared for the Lord. The wonderful outpouring of material means and benevolent labors which we have witnessed of

late years in America, to re-establish our Union,
and to mitigate the horrors of war, would be emu·
lated and exceeded over the whole world, by the
manner in which Christ's people would "come up
to the help of the Lord against the mighty."

There has never been such a missionary church
in the world as that of the two first centuries of
the Christian era, and if there is any truth in his·
tory, that church was thoroughly millenarian. Mosheim, in his church history, although opposed to
this doctrine, says, "Long before this controversy,
an opinion had prevailed that Christ was to come
and reign a thousand years among men before the
entire and final destruction of the world; this
opinion had hitherto" (that is, down to the middle
of the third century, of which time he was writing) "met with no opposition. But in this century its credit began to decline, principally through
the influence and authority of Origen, who opposed
it with the greatest warmth, because it was incompatible with some of his most favorite sentiments."

I have given some specimens of Origen's mode
of interpreting Scripture in the beginning of the
third chapter. Mosheim denounces his system as
"wild, fanciful, chimerical, mystical, licentious."

Dr. Clarke, in his Sacred Literature, says, "that
on his plan of interpretation, the sacred writings
may be obliged to say anything, everything, or
nothing, according to the fancy, peculiar creed, or
caprice of the interpreter." No wonder he was

5   6*

able to explain away whatever was *incompatible with his favorite sentiments.*

Gibbon tells us, " the ancient and popular doctrine of the Millennium was intimately connected *with the second coming of Christ.* The assurance of such a Millennium was carefully inculcated by a succession of fathers, from Justin Martyr and Irenæus, who conversed with the immediate disciples of the apostles, down to Lactantius, who was preceptor to the son of Constantine. Though it might not have been universally received, it appears to have been the reigning sentiment of the orthodox believers ; and it seems so well adapted to the desires and apprehensions of mankind, that it must have contributed in a very considerable degree to the progress of the Christian faith. But when the edifice of the church was almost completed, the temporary support was laid aside. The doctrine of Christ's reign on the earth was first treated as a profound allegory, was considered by degrees as a doubtful and useless opinion, and was at length rejected as the absurd invention of heresy and fanaticism. A mysterious prophecy which still forms a part of the sacred canon, but which was thought to favor the exploded sentiment, has very narrowly escaped the proscription of the church."

Biblical students must have remarked the fact, thus insinuated by the learned infidel historian, viz., that the Apocalypse was universally acknowledged to be canonical in the primitive church ; but that its authority was disputed in the latter part of the third, and the beginning of the fourth, century, since which time there has been no dispute in regard to its inspiration and authenticity. Gibbon in the above passage has hinted at the reason. Ante-millenarianism, which was first heard of in the third century, although able, by Origen's system of "spiritualization," to explain away other portions of Scripture, came to a dead lock on the twentieth chapter of Revelations, and could devise no mode of removing the difficulty short of striking the whole book from the canon. Let us see what Dr. Joseph Addison Alexander, one of the most learned men Princeton has produced, says on this subject. I quote his notes on "New Testament Literature." Speaking of the Apocalypse, he writes, "The main fact here is, that in tracing the books upward, after finding this one undisputed at the close of the fourth century, we come first to vague intimations, then to positive assertions, and at last to argumentative attempts at demostrations, that it cannot be canonical; but passing on still further, we discover it completely reinstated, and the recognition of it more or less distinctly running back to the very age of the Apostles. In other words, the book was at first received by all, then suspected or condemned by some, and then again unanimously recognized as genuine." After explaining the reason for its omission in one of the ancient versions, he continues, "A no less plausible and even satisfactory solution of the other fact in reference to this book, viz., its exclusion from the canon by some fathers of the third and fourth centuries, is furnished by the well known circumstance, that chiliastic (*i.e.* Millenarian) doctrines of a very gross form then extensively prevailed, though constantly repudiated by the church at large, and so abhorred by some distinguished teachers, that it tempted them to sweep away its alleged foundation, by discrediting the part of Scripture which contained it."

From the language of this learned Professor it therefore appears, that some of the so-called "fathers of the church," in order to put down a fanatical perversion of a glorious doctrine, attempted to root out the doctrine itself; and could find no possible mode of doing so, except by striking from the Bible the very portion of the volume which closes with the awful anathema, "If any man shall take away from the words of the book of this prophecy, God shall take away his part out of the book of life, and out of the holy city, and from the things that are written in this book. He that testifieth these things saith, Surely I come quickly: Amen! even so come Lord Jesus." May we not say in regard to such Church fathers, "Ye blind guides! that strain at a gnat, and swallow a camel."

The late Bishop Henshaw, of Rhode Island, in his work on the Second Advent, declared that "the commonly received opinion of a spiritual

Millennium, consisting in a universal triumph of the Gospel, and the conversion of all nations for a thousand years, before the coming of Christ, *is a novel doctrine, unknown to the Church for the space of sixteen hundred years.* So far as we have been able to investigate its history, it was first advanced by the Rev. Dr. Whitby, the commentator." "We may safely challenge its advocates to produce one distinguished writer in its favor, who lived before the commencement of the eighteenth century." Dr. Whitby's commentary was published in 1710. He himself claimed originality of discovery in regard to this doctrine as "a new hypothesis." In proposing it, he acknowledged that the Pre-Millennial Advent was believed and taught in the early Church, by "the best of Christians for 250 years as a doctrine Apostolical." If the Encyclopedia Americana be correct, which says that before his death he adopted the Arian heresy, his hypotheses ought not to have much weight with orthodox Christians.

Martin Luther declared, "Some say that before the latter days, the whole world shall become Christians. This is a falsehood of Satan, that he might darken sound doctrine. Beware, therefore, of this delusion."

John Knox said of this world's universal reform: "It never was nor yet shall be, till that righteous King and Judge appear for the restoration of all things."

John Calvin wrote: "There is no reason why any person should expect the conversion of the world; for at length (when it will be too late, and yield them no advantage), they shall look on Him whom they have pierced."

And yet, notwithstanding all this, I have heard a learned divine denounce from the pulpit, the doctrine of the Pre-Millennial advent as "a modern dogma, which cannot be true, unless the words of Christ are false."

Much harm has been done by the ill-regulated enthusiasm of some preachers and writers, who have attempted too confidently to fix the times and seasons, which the Father has kept secret. In the year 1000, A.D., there was so general a belief in some parts of Europe that the end was at hand, that the fields were left untilled, people neglected their ordinary employments, and great suffering ensued in consequence. The fanaticism of the Anabaptists of Luther's time, and of the Fifth Monarchy men in the days of Cromwell, are sad instances of the perversion of this doctrine, and such may have been the case in regard to the Chiliasts, of whom Dr. Alexander speaks in the third century. But what doctrine of the Bible has not been perverted by fanatics? Has it not been declared that there are non-elect infants in hell, not a span long? Have not pretended saints, while guilty of shameful licentiousness, declared that to the pure all things are pure, and that being born of God they could not commit sin? Will Calvinists, on this account, reject their doctrines of election and the perseverance of the saints?

The writer of a book published in 1862, undertook not only to prove that Louis Napoleon is the personal Antichrist, but that he would make a covenant with the Jews in 1863, and restore them to their own land; that Christ will come in 1870, descending at Armageddon, and closing this dispensation. He admitted, however, the possibility of these dates being a year or two in error; and in a subsequent edition postponed these events to 1865 and 1872.

About twenty years ago a preacher in this city convinced himself and many others that the Lord would certainly come on a particular day, and it is said that many persons at the appointed time went out into the fields, with white ascension robes which they had prepared, and waited to be caught up in the air.

Other dates have been assigned with more or less confidence by different writers, some of which are past, and most of the remainder culminate within the next ten years. Examination of them has not satisfied me that human wisdom has discovered the key of the mystery. Of this, however, I am sure, for the mouth of the Lord hath spoken it. "Of that day knoweth no man, no, not the angels of heaven, but my Father only. But as the days of Noah were, so shall also the coming of the

Son of man be. For as in the days that were before the flood, they were eating and drinking,
marrying, and giving in marriage, until the day
that Noah entered into the ark, and knew not until
the flood came and took them all away; so shall
also the coming of the Son of man be. Then shall
two be in the field; the one shall be taken and the
other left. Two women shall be grinding at the
mill; the one shall be taken and the other left."
"And take heed to yourselves lest at any time
your hearts be overcharged with surfeiting and
drunkenness, and cares of this life, and so that day
come upon you unawares. For as a snare shall it
come *on all them that dwell on the face of the whole
earth.* Watch ye, therefore, and pray always that
ye may be accounted worthy to escape all these
things that shall come to pass, and to stand before
the Son of man." If any one shall satisfy me that
these plain and emphatic words of the Son of God
only mean that we must all die, or the destruction
of Jerusalem, or the destruction of the world, or
anything else except the actual personal coming
of the Lord himself to close this dispensation, I
shall almost be compelled to acknowledge that
Origen was a sound expositor of Scripture, and
consequently that Talleyrand was correct in his
declaration, that "the chief use of language is to
conceal our ideas."

I pretend not to know when the Lord will come;
but he has told us to be always ready, waiting and

watching for his appearing. The signs of the times seem to promise, that, even within the lives of some of us,. this dispensation may come to an end. Improbable as the restoration of the Jews to their own land now appears to many, I venture to say that the total abolition of slavery in the United States seemed even more unlikely five years since.

The year before Louis Napoleon seized the imperial purple, I stood in the garden of the Tuilleries and witnessed the imposing spectacle of the National Guards reviewed by the Prince President. A French gentleman at my side asked me if I had ever seen such a sight in America. I answered, "No, and I trust in God such a sight will never be seen there as 46,000 men under arms." I would then have much more readily believed in the restoration of the Jews in 1864, than that a million and a half of veteran soldiers would have been slaughtering each other in my beloved country in that year, and that in a single twelve months' campaign of one of the armies fighting on our soil for the support of the Union, its losses in killed, wounded, and missing would amount by official statement to nearly double the entire host which Louis Napoleon reviewed on that day.

Railroads, steamships, and telegraphs have made things possible by natural means which would have required miracles in the last century. Science, labor, and capital have pierced mountains by tunnels,. bridged great gorges, and straightened tortuous valleys for the passage of the locomotive, seeming literally to fulfil the prediction of Isaiah in regard to the Advent. "Every valley shall be exalted, and every mountain and hill shall be made low; and the crooked shall be made straight, and the rough places plain."

Before Livingston, and Barth, and Speke had penetrated and traversed the great Continent of Africa, which had so long been marked on our maps as terra incognita, how could we have fulfilled the command to preach the gospel to all nations? How strangely the explorations of these men under the blazing sun, and exposed to the withering diseases of the tropics, unite with those of Parry, Franklin, Kane, and others whose sufferings and dangers in the Arctic regions freeze the very blood of those who read their adventures; and all point us to Daniel's prophecy, that in "the time of the end many shall run to and fro, and knowledge shall be increased?" Is it not time to "stablish your hearts, for the coming of the Lord draweth nigh."

> "We are living, we are dwelling
>   In a grand eventful time;
> In an age on ages telling,
>   To be living is sublime.
>
> "Hark! the waking up of nations,
>   Truth and error to the fray;
> Hark! what soundeth? 'tis creation
>   Groaning for its latter day.

"Will ye play then? will ye dally
  With your music and your wine?
Up! it is Jehovah's rally,
  God's own arm has need of thine.

"Hark, the onset! will ye fold your
  Faith-clad arms in lazy lock?
Up! oh, up! thou drowsy soldier,
  Worlds are charging to the shock.

"Worlds are charging, heaven beholding!
  Thou hast but an hour to fight;
Now the blazoned cross unfolding,
  On! right onward for the right."
                              A. C. COXE.

CHAPTER VII.

TESTIMONY OF THE PRIMITIVE CHURCH.—PRE, ANTI, AND POST-
MILLENARIANISM.—APOSTOLIC AND MODERN PREACHING ON
CHRIST'S COMING CONTRASTED.—PRE-MILLENNIAL HYMNS AND
POETRY.—CONCLUSION.

THE doctrine of the Pre-Millennial Advent, can,
of course, only be proved by Scripture, and
its advocates desire to rest it on no other foundation. It cannot however be denied that in ques-
tions of doubtful interpretation, the views of the
Apostolical fathers, who derived their knowledge
from the Apostles themselves, or their immediate
followers, are worthy of very respectful consideration. Among the most distinguished of these
ranks Justin Martyr, born A.D. 89, and martyred
A.D. 163. He was·not only a decided pre-millenarian, but distinctly declared that all orthodox and
right-minded Christians believed as he did on this
important subject, and denied those who rejected it
to be Christians at all; the fact being that none
but actual heretics did deny it in his time. It is
hardly worth while however to multiply the names
of these ancient worthies, for infidel and post-
millenarian authorities alike acknowledge that

this was the faith of the orthodox primitive church. It was, indeed, the faith which sustained the early martyrs in their bitter sufferings; that they might be esteemed worthy of a part in the first resurrection, and reign with their Lord in his millennial glory. Rev. 20 : 4 to 6 — "And I saw thrones, and they that sat on them, and judgment was given to them; and I saw the souls of them that were beheaded for the witness of Jesus, and for the word of God, and which had not worshipped the beast, neither his image, neither had received his mark upon their foreheads or in their hands; and they lived and reigned with Christ a thousand years. But the rest of the dead lived not again, until the thousand years were finished. Blessed and holy is he that hath part in the first resurrection; on such the second death hath no power, but they shall be priests of God and of Christ, and shall reign with him a thousand years."

I believe that a careful and impartial study of church history will fully establish three facts:

1. The orthodox, Apostolic church was pre-millenarian; and I mean by this, they believed that Christ would come a second time, and reign personally a thousand years; which would be a golden age of peace, happiness, and righteousness.

2. Anti - millenarianism first took form and power, if indeed it was not first invented, in the third century. Its followers denied the millennium altogether, denounced it as a Jewish fable, and

7*

endeavored to strike the Apocalypse from the Bible, because it clearly taught this doctrine.

. 3. Post-millenarianism (the doctrine now prevalent in the Protestant Churches, which promises a spiritual millennium to be produced by causes now at work, which shall gradually extend Christianity over the whole earth; which millennium is to precede Christ's second personal advent) was never heard of in the primitive church; was unknown or denied as false by Calvin, Luther, and Knox; is not embodied in the confessions of faith, articles of religion, or platforms of any Evangelical denomination of Protestants; but is the modern discovery of an English Episcopalian, himself strongly suspected of unsoundness · on other points acknowledged to be essential by all orthodox churches.

Whatever else may be charged against premillenarianism, none can truthfully assert that it is a "new hypothesis," or a "modern dogma." It is at least as old as the Bible, and it is high time for its opponents to acknowledge both its venerable antiquity, and the respectability of its sponsors.

I solemnly protest against the customary and frivolous fashion of pretending that the mistakes of commentators about the date of the Second Advent, afford any proof that this event will not be pre-millennial. The Thessalonians supposed that the Second Advent was to be immediate; and St. Paul warned them that this was a mistake, as

certain events must occur before Christ's appearing.
We have no St. Paul now to correct the errors
which Mede, Newton, Fleming, and Elliott may
have made; but their mistakes, if ascertained to
be such, no more disprove this doctrine, than did
the Thessalonian error above referred to. We all
profess to believe in a millennium, and in a
second personal advent; and the real question at
issue is, which of these is to come first? If this
question shall be fully and fairly investigated on
Scriptural grounds alone, the result seems to me
to be inevitable, that our clergy must joyfully
return to the Apostolical encouragements and
warnings, which are so rarely heard at present
from our pulpits. Listen to some of them. "The
Lord cometh." "The Lord is at hand." "I pray
God, your whole spirit and soul and body, be preserved blameless unto the coming of our Lord
Jesus Christ." "And the Lord direct your hearts
into the love of God, and into the patient waiting
for Christ." "Keep this commandment without
spot, unrebukable, until the appearing of our
Lord Jesus Christ." "Looking for that blessed
hope, and the glorious appearing of the great God,
and our Saviour Jesus Christ." "Unto them that
look for Him, shall He appear the second time,
without sin unto salvation." "Yet a little while,
and He that shall come, will come and will not
tarry." "Be patient, therefore, brethren unto the
coming of the Lord." "Be ye also patient; stab-

lish your hearts; for the coming of the Lord
draweth nigh." "Behold the judge standeth at
the door." "So that ye come behind in no gift;
waiting for the coming of our Lord Jesus Christ,
who shall also confirm you unto the end, that ye
may be blameless in the day of our Lord Jesus
Christ." "Looking for and hasting unto the day
of God." "Abide in Him, that, when He shall
appear, we may have confidence, and not be
ashamed before Him at his coming." And now
look at the last utterances of our Lord himself to
His Apostle John: "I will put upon you none
other burden but that which ye have already, hold
fast till I come." "If therefore thou shalt not
watch, I will come upon thee as a thief, and thou
shalt not know what hour I will come upon thee."
"Behold I come quickly! hold fast that which
thou hast, that no man take thy crown." "Behold
I come as a thief! blessed is he that watcheth and
keepeth his garments." "Behold I come quickly!
blessed is he that keepeth the sayings of the
prophecy of this book." "Behold I come quickly!
and my reward is with me." "He who testifieth
these things saith, surely I come quickly!"

I declare, without fear of contradiction, that the
great argument of the Apostles to Christians, in
favor of holiness of life, and patience under perse-
cutions and afflictions, was the certain coming of
Christ; their most terrible warning to those who
did not love Christ, was "Maranatha," the Lord

cometh. The crowning encouragement of our
blessed Lord himself to his followers, to persevere
in purity and watchfulness was, "Surely I come
quickly." In short, *the coming of Christ was the
hope of the Apostolic Church.* Is it so now? Can
any one truthfully affirm, that the coming of the
Lord holds such a place in modern preaching as it
did in the Apostolic epistles? As a general rule,
do we ever hear it from the pulpit, unless it hap-
pens to be part of a chapter read for some other
purpose? and if expounded, are we not usually
warned, either directly or by implication, that it
means something else? And if this is the case,
and I am sure that I have not intentionally over-
stated the fact, may we not reasonably infer that
the Apostles who were inspired by the Holy Spirit,
were right, and that the Church has fallen into
error, under the impression that "the Lord delayeth
his coming?"

It is very difficult to cast off the habit into which
we have been educated, of interpreting these truths
in a figurative sense. I have often wondered that
others did not look upon them in the same light
that I did; but never more than in the perusal of
a book written by one whom I have good cause to
love and revere as a dear Christian friend. In this
work the author, after speaking of the coming kingdom of God in the usual manner, and treating it as
entirely spiritual, closes his remarks on this point
with two of Horatius Bonar's beautiful pre-millen-

6

nial hymns, which were written under the deepest
conviction of their literal truth and speedy fulfilment; and he gives not the slightest intimation that
any other than a figurative meaning can be attached
to the words.   This seemed to me passing strange;
but when I reflected that the thoughts, language,
and imagery of these hymns are eminently scriptural, and that every thing that they contain is
found just as clearly in the Bible, I ceased to
wonder. We have been taught to look upon the
prophecies as if they were all written in cypher,
and needed some ingenious commentator's key to
enable us to understand them, and of course their
paraphrases are treated in the same manner.   We
do not really believe such hymns as these:

COME, LORD.

Senuit mundus. — AUGUSTINE.

Come, Lord, and tarry not,
  Bring the long looked-for day;
Oh, why these years of waiting here —
  These ages of delay?

Come, for thy saints still wait,
  Daily ascends their sigh;
The Spirit and the Bride say, Come!
  Dost thou not hear the cry?

Come, for creation groans,
  Impatient of thy stay;
Worn out with these long years of ill,
  These ages of delay.

Come, for thy Israel pines,
  An exile from thy fold;
O call to mind thy faithful word,
  And bless them, as of old.

Come, for thy foes are strong,
  With taunting lip they say:
"Where is the promised Advent now,
  And where the dreaded day?"

Come, for the good are few,
  They lift the voice in vain;
Faith waxes fainter on the earth,
  And love is on the wane.

Come, for the truth is weak,
  And error pours abroad
Its subtle poison o'er the earth,—
  An earth that hates her God.

Come, for love waxes cold,
  Its steps are faint and slow;
Faith now is lost in unbelief,
  Hope's lamp burns dim and low.

Come, for the grave is full,
  Earth's tombs no more can hold
The sated sepulchres rebel,
  And groans the heaving mould.

Come, for the corn is ripe,
  Put in thy sickle now,
Reap the great harvest of the earth,
  Sower and reaper thou!

Come, in thy glorious might,
  Come, with the iron rod;
Scattering thy foes before thy face,
  Most mighty Son of God!

Come, spoil the strong man's house,
  Bind him, and cast him hence;
Show thyself stronger than the strong,
  Thyself Omnipotence.

Come, and make all things new,
  Build up this ruined earth;
Restore our faded Paradise,
  Creation's second birth.

Come, and begin thy reign
  Of everlasting peace;
Come, take the kingdom to thyself,
  Great King of righteousness.

                              H. BONAR.

———

ADVENT.

The church has waited long,
  Her absent Lord to see;
And still in loneliness she waits,
  A friendless stranger she.
Age after age has gone,
  Sun after sun has set,
And still, in weeds of widowhood,
  She weeps, a mourner yet.
      Come, then, Lord Jesus, come.

Saint after saint on earth
  Has lived, and loved, and died;
And as they left us one by one,
  We laid them side by side;
We laid them down to sleep,
  But not in hope forlorn;
We laid them but to ripen there,
  Till the last glorious morn.
      Come, then, Lord Jesus, come!

The serpent's brood increase,
  The powers of hell grow bold,
The conflict thickens, faith is low,
  And love is waxing cold.
How long, O Lord our God,
  Holy, and true, and good,
Wilt thou not judge thy suffering Church,
  Her sighs, and tears, and blood?
      Come, then, Lord Jesus, come!

We long to hear thy voice,
  To see thee face to face,
To share thy crown and glory then,
  As now we share thy grace.
Should not the loving bride
  The absent bridegroom mourn?
Should she not wear the weeds of grief,
  Until her Lord return?
      Come, then, Lord Jesus, come!

The whole creation groans,
  And waits to hear that voice
That shall restore her comeliness,
  And make her wastes rejoice;

Come, Lord, and wipe away
The curse, the sin, the stain,
And make this blighted world of ours
Thine own fair world again.
Come, then, Lord Jesus, come!

H. BONAR.

It hardly occurs to us that Heber was in serious earnest when he wrote the following:

Yes, Salem, thou shalt rise: thy Father's aid
Shall heal the wounds his chastening hand has made;
Shall judge the proud oppressor's ruthless sway,
And burst his brazen bonds, and cast his cords away.
Then on your tops shall deathless verdure spring;
Break forth, ye mountains, and ye valleys sing!
No more your thirsty rocks shall frown forlorn—
The unbeliever's jest, the heathen's scorn;
The sultry sands shall tenfold harvests yield,
And a new Eden deck the thorny field—
E'en now perchance, wide waving o'er the land,
That mighty angel lifts his golden wand,
Courts the bright vision of ascending power,
Tells every gate, and measures every tower;
And chides the tardy seals that yet detain
Thy Lion Judah, from his destined reign!
And who is He? the vast, the awful form,
Girt with the whirlwind, sandaled with the storm!
A western cloud around his limbs is spread,
His crown a rainbow, and a sun his head;
To highest heaven he lifts his kingly hand,
And treads at once the ocean and the land;
And hark! his voice amid the thunders roar,
His dreadful voice, that time shall be no more.

Lo! cherub hands the golden courts prepare,
Lo! thrones arise, and every saint is there;
Earth's utmost bounds confess their awful sway,
The mountains worship, and the isles obey;
Nor sun nor moon they need, nor day nor night;
God is their temple, and the Lamb their light;
And shall not Israel's sons exulting come,
Hail the glad beam, and claim their ancient home?
On David's throne shall David's offspring reign,
And the dry bones be warm with life again.
Hark! white robed crowds their deep hosannas raise,
And the hoarse flood repeats the sound of praise;
Ten thousand harps attune the mystic song,
Ten thousand thousand saints the strain prolong;
"Worthy the Lamb! omnipotent to save,
Who died, who lives, triumphant o'er the grave."

Read the Advent hymns of this Missionary
Bishop and Christian poet, and see if he was
not in earnest on this subject. Here is one of
them :

The world is grown old, and her pleasures are past;
The world is grown old, and her form may not last;
The world is grown old, and trembles for fear;
For sorrows abound, and judgment is near!

The sun in the heaven is languid and pale;
And feeble and few are the fruits of the vale;
And the hearts of the nations fail them for fear,
For the world is grown old, and judgment is near!

The King on his Throne, the Bride in her bower,
The children of pleasure all feel the sad hour;
The roses are faded, and tasteless the cheer,
For the world is grown old, and judgment is near!

The world is grown old! but should we complain,
Who have tried her and know that her promise is vain?
Our heart is in heaven, our home is not here,
And we look for our crown, when the judgment is near.

———

Here is another:

In the sun and moon and stars
    Signs and wonders there shall be:
Earth shall quake with inward wars,
    Nations with perplexity.

Soon shall Ocean's hoary deep
    Tossed with stronger tempests rise;
Darker storms the mountain sweep,
    Redder lightning rend the skies.

Evil thoughts shall shake the proud,
    Racking doubt and endless fear;
And amid the thunder cloud
    Shall the Judge of men appear.

But though from that awful face
    Heaven shall fade and earth shall fly,
Fear not ye, His chosen race,
    Your redemption draweth nigh!

The hymn book at my hand is that of the Pres-
byterian Church, New School, and I find in it such
hymns as these:

> When shall the voice of singing
>   Flow joyfully along?
> When hill and valley, ringing
>   With one triumphant song,
> Proclaim the contest ended,
>   And Him who once was slain,
> Again to earth descended
>   In righteousness to reign.

> Hasten, Lord! the promised hour;
> Come in glory and in power;
> Still thy foes are unsubdued,
> Nature sighs to be renewed.
> Time has nearly reached its sum,
> All things with the bride say "Come!"
> Jesus! whom all worlds adore,
> Come! and reign for evermore.

> Behold on flying clouds he comes,
>   And every eye shall see him move;
> Though with our sins we pierced him once,
>   Still he displays his pardoning love.
> The unbelieving world shall wail,
>   While we rejoice to see the day;
> Come Lord! nor let thy promise fail,
>   Nor let thy chariot long delay.

8*

It would be a sad "index expurgatorius" that would erase the pre-millenarian hymns from our books of praise. It is to be regretted that more of them do not find place there, for many which are omitted breathe the most holy, fervent, and reverential spirit.

I have now finished the task which I undertook to perform, though, so far from being exhausted, the theme has only been commenced. I only proposed, in a short and elementary manner, to introduce the subject to those who have hitherto neglected it as a useless speculation, or rejected it as a fanatical perversion of the truth. I hoped to induce them to examine the subject further by the light that abler and more learned teachers can supply; or far better to make the investigation by the light supplied by God himself in his own blessed word. Much of the Bible is virtually sealed to the laity by the mode in which it is expounded. It is an irksome and unprofitable task to read to our children the prophecies which form so large a part of it, under the necessity of constantly explaining to them that the language means something else. When I first found a Christian pastor, whom I personally knew to be learned, intelligent, and godly, actually believing and teaching that *the Word of God is true as it stands;* that Israel, Jacob, Judah, and Ephraim *mean the Jews,* and not the Christians; that Christ's coming means *Christ's coming,* and not merely death or the de-

struction of Jerusalem ; and that Messiah sitting
on the throne of David and ruling over his people
Israel, means that *Christ is to be the King of the
Jews,* and not only ruler in Christian hearts ; it was
a great relief and comfort to me, and I hope and
pray that this humble essay may bring like relief
and comfort to others.

Dr. Franklin once addressed to the Parisians a
paper entitled " An Economical Project," in which
he explained to them as an important discovery
made by himself, that the sun actually rises at the
time designated in the almanacs, and that consequently an immense sum could be saved in Paris
in the cost of lamps and candles, if every body
would rise early in the morning and go to bed as
soon as it is dark. His essay concludes thus : " It
is impossible that so sensible a people, under such
circumstances, should have lived so long by the
smoky, unwholesome, and unpleasant light of
candles, if they had really known that they might
have had as much pure light of the sun for
nothing."

And, so I may say, it is wonderful that an
intelligent Christian people will close their eyes
to the pure light of the Word of God, and be satisfied with the dim, misty, dreary tapers with which
commentators endeavor to make darkness visible.

I close with the eloquent appeal of an eminent
servant of God, whom I have more than once

quoted already; but he says what I wish to say in more forcible language than I can command.

"They greatly err who suppose that our doctrine is based on a few knotty and doubtful texts. The passages on which it rests, and on the strength of which we ask the reader to hesitate before he rejects it, are neither few nor ambiguous. They give forth no uncertain sound, no feeble, no inarticulate utterance. Their testimony is not scanty and infrequent, but full and oft-repeated. No other doctrine can produce a larger, more distinct, and more vigorous testimony in its favor. Many of the truths which we receive as incontestible are built upon a basis by no means so solid or so broad as this. Its witnesses are very numerous and worthy of being listened to. It pervades the whole Word of God, from Genesis to Revelations. It is not confined to the figurative books; it declares itself with equal fulness in narrative and epistle, as in symbol and type. Like a thread of gold it runs through the whole web of revelation, crossing and recrossing it everywhere, and imparting the richest brilliance to the whole texture. It is the burden of all prophecy. It is the summing up, as well as the unravelling of all history. It is the final and grand solution of the mystery of God's dealings with this world of ours. It is the germ of Israel's types. It is woven into all their ordinances, and rites, and festivals. It is the theme of many a Psalm; the heart of many a symbol; the subject of many a parable; the end and point of many a promise; the seal set to the 'Gospel of the grace of God as the 'Gospel of the kingdom,' that is the good news concerning the open gate for sinners into that kingdom prepared from the foundation of the world !

" It has been the *hope of the Church* through many a starless night, when other hopes had gone out one by one, like beacons shattered by the tempest, leaving her disconsolate and helpless. It is now again, in our day, pressed upon her notice, as her strength in 'the hour of temptation which is coming upon all the world;' the only light which cannot be quenched, and by which she will be able to steer her perilous course through the gloom of the thickening storm.

"It is no dream of carnal enthusiasts, enamored of materialism, and anticipating a paradise of gross delights. It is the calm belief of spiritual men, resting on God's sure promise, and looking forward to a kingdom of 'righteousness, and peace, and joy in the Holy Ghost.' It is no hasty conjecture, no novelty of a feverish age, rashly caught up, without consideration and without evidence. It can produce the testimony of ages in its behalf; and they who have held it in our day, have been men who have studied the Bible on their knees, and have come to their conclusions after long, deliberate, and most solemn investigation. It is no fable of romance; it is sober scriptural reality, though far beyond what fancy ever painted. It is no vision of the politician; yet it shows us how, ere long, shall be exemplified that which earthly governments have been vainly striving to realize, a peaceful and a prosperous world. It is no creation of the intellect; the wisdom of this intellectual age rejects it as foolishness, and rationalism resents it as one of the exploded fancies of unenlightened criticism. It is no popular theory of the many; there are comparatively few in the Churches who receive it — few who will even concede to it a place among the things which deserve serious study, or are accessible to proof. Yet all are concerned in it; and it comes abroad proclaiming itself alike to the Church of God and to the heedless multitude, as the consummation towards which the various lines of prophecy are rapidly converging, as the glorious issue of all the confusion, the sin, the change, the death, that have made earth so long a wilderness, as the only cure for those deep and manifold evils under which men are groaning, and which they are so earnestly, yet so vainly, striving to remedy."

I will not weaken Dr. Bonar's words by anything more of my own. May God bless what I have written, in so far as it has been in accordance with His truth. AMEN.